Math  Kids

presents

The Country of the Tens

RODOLFO VILLICAÑA

An interesting story that tells us about the adventures of the units on their school trip that they made to the Land of the Tens. With this story, children will learn in a fun way the differences between units and tens, and how a unit can be transformed into a ten.

All the students of the teacher Mily are very excited because we are going to take a trip to the Land of the Tens.

After a long journey we reached the border. At that time there were already very long lines to enter the Country of the Tens, so the teacher Mily asked us never to leave the line, because the units had to enter through a special door.

BUS
STOP

The teacher Mily was explaining to us that the units can only pass to the Country of the Tens through the door of the Addition (+) or through the door of the Multiplication (X)

In an oversight on the part of the teacher, while she was explaining how we were going to enter, the Number Nine and the Number Three entered the Country of the Tens through the door of the Addition (+).

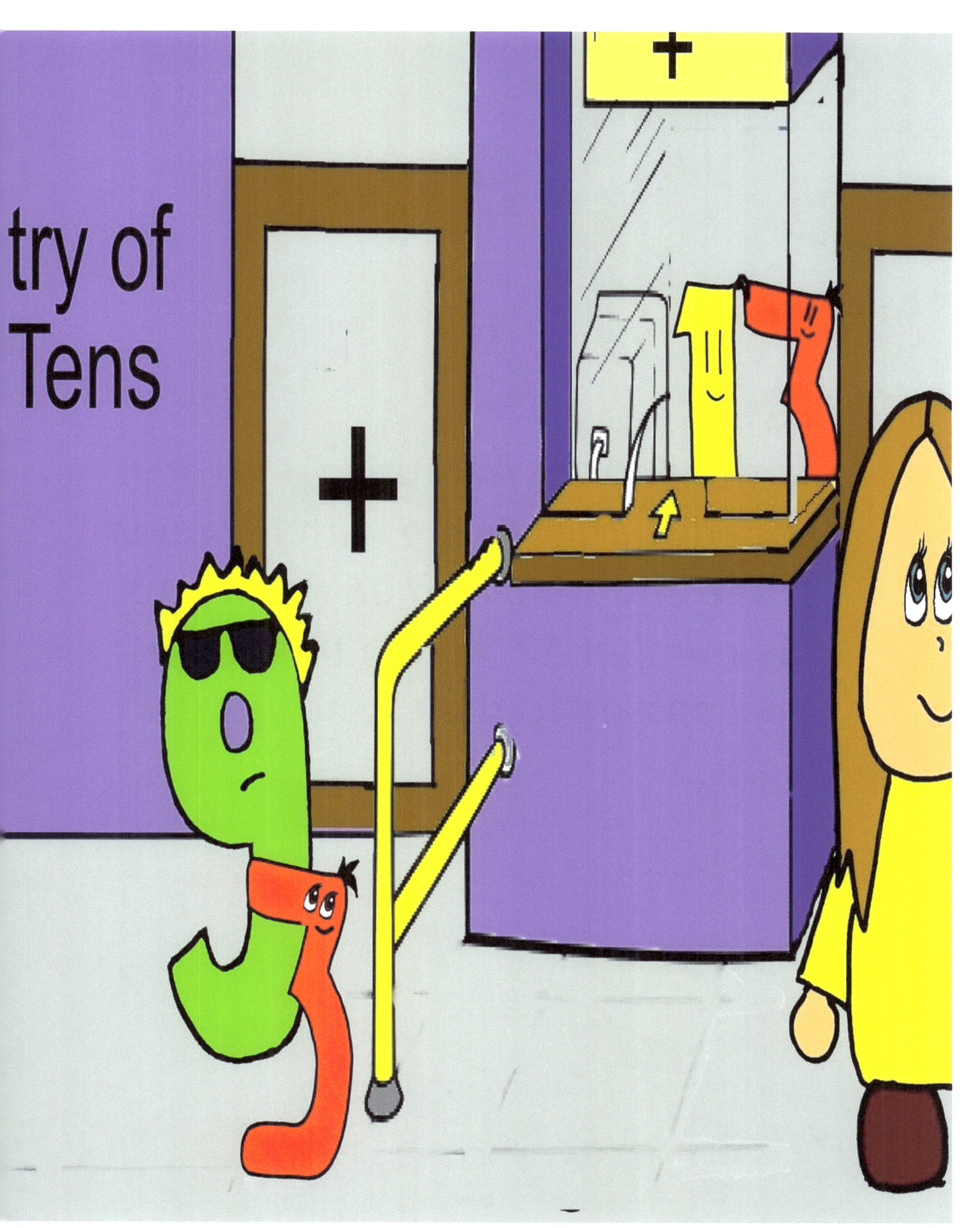
try of
Tens

At the door of Addition (+), they added Number Nine with Number Three and transformed them into the number 12, and in this way, they passed to the country of 2 digits.

The teacher told us to make a row from smallest to largest and it was when the teacher realized that Number Three and Number Nine were missing.

BUS
STOP

The teacher immediately notified the police. A plus sign in charge of the adding machine said that a number 3 and a number 9 had passed through that door. The police from the Land of Tens started looking for them and 1-hour later they located them playing in a park.

They were immediately taken to the border to be returned to the Country of the Units with their teacher Mily. To return to Number Three with the rest of the group, they had to subtract number 9 from Number 12.

Then number 3 was subtracted from the number 12 and so Number Nine returned to us again. The teacher scolded the 2 disobedient numbers and told them not to leave the group again if they want to be admitted to go to another school field trip again.

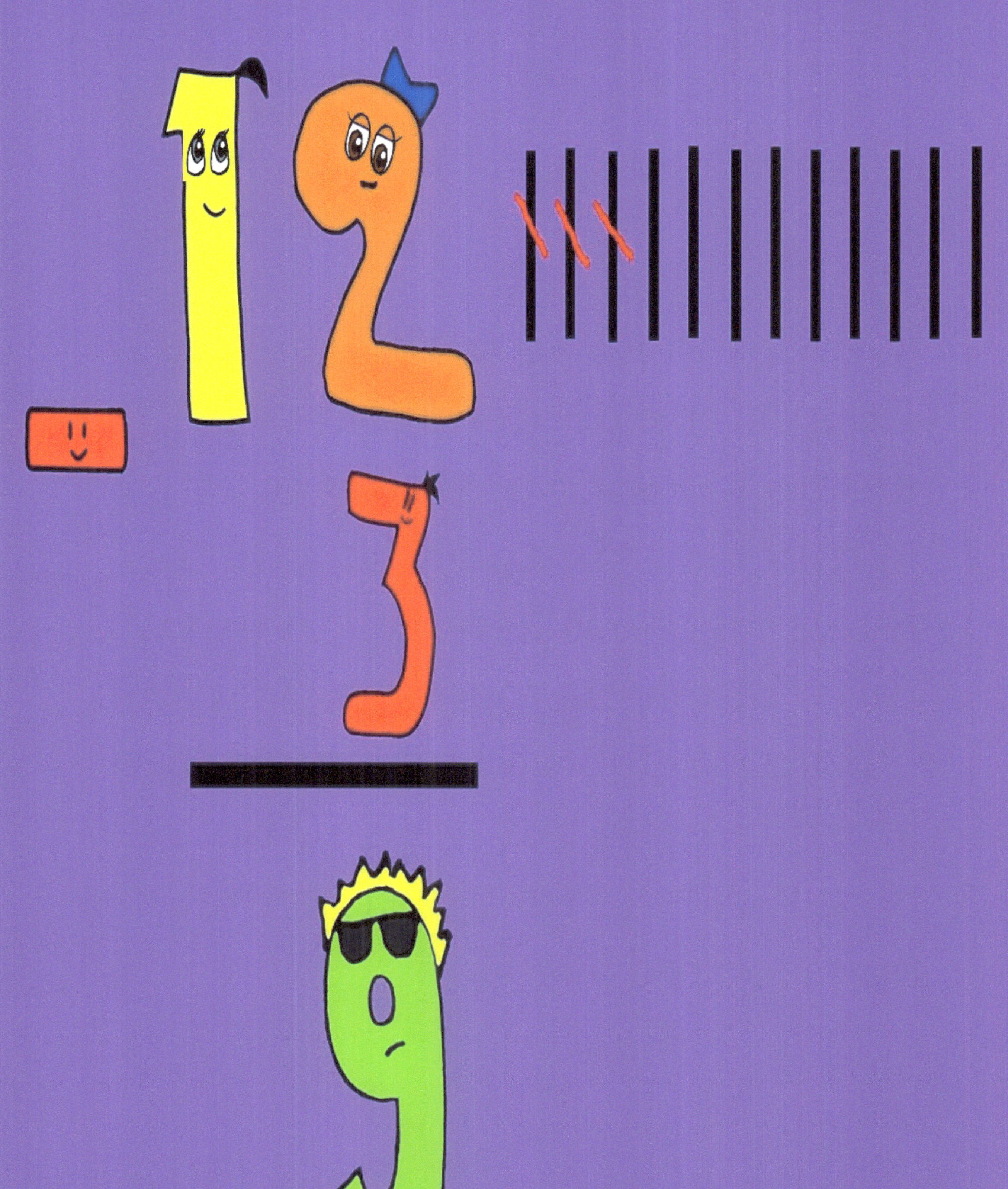

In order to move to the country of 2 digits, the border agents multiplied each of the units by 11. In other words, they made us 11 times bigger. When we got out of the multiplying machine, we came out accompanied by a dozen who looked like us but were 10 times bigger. All the tens next to the units looked like giants.

After we got out of the multiplying machine, the teacher took several pictures of us to keep as souvenirs.

 After leaving the multiplying machine, we were passed through another machine that made all the numbers the same size. Since in the Country of Tens it is the law that all numbers must be of the same height even if they have different values because it is very difficult to walk and work all the time with a ten that is 10 times higher than the unit.

The first thing that surprised us in the country of 2 digits is that all numbers always go in pairs. On the left side there always located the tens and on the right side always the units.

All the houses were very large with very wide doors. All the swings and chairs had 2 places together. And all the bikes had 2 seats. In the land of tens, everything is designed for two numbers together!

A bus took us to an amusement park and all numbers were very excited. But soon I started having trouble coming to terms with my ten. When I wanted to play one game, my ten wanted to play another game. And the bad thing is that by law we can never separate

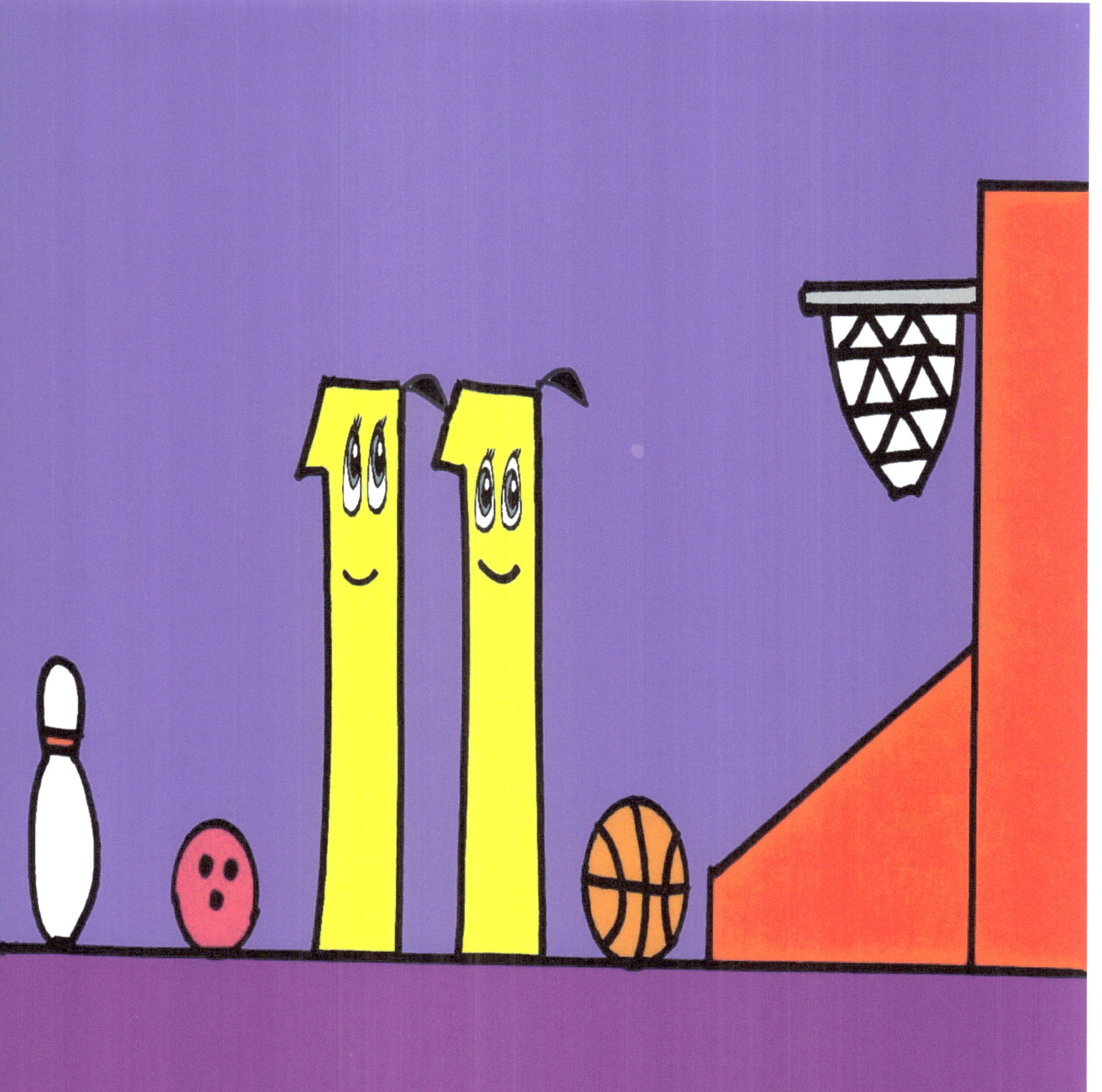

My ten were very good in all the games and he did everything 10 times better and faster than me. When we bowled while I bowled one pin my ten bowled 10 pins. And when we played basketball, I only made one basket and my ten made 10 baskets.

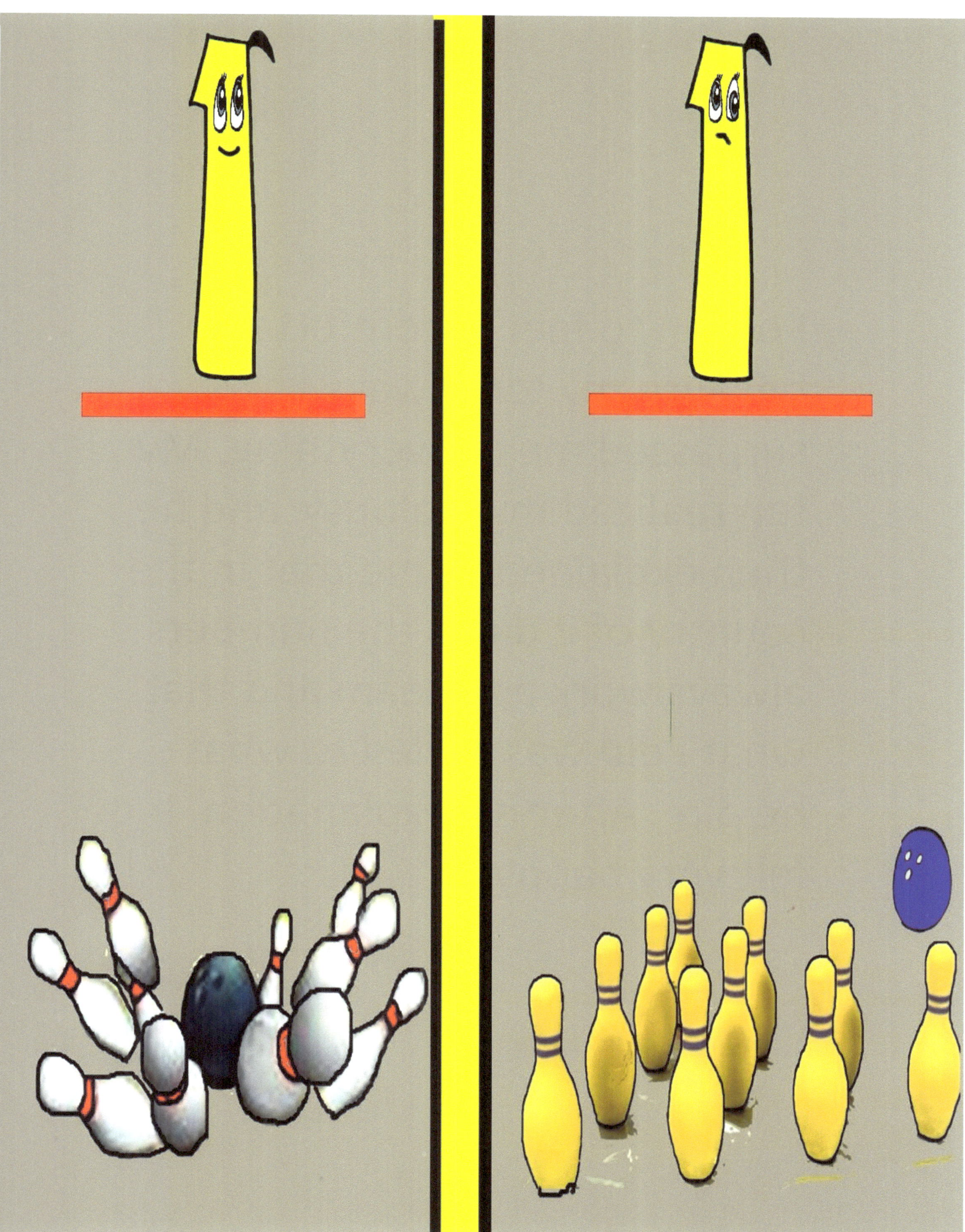

I began to feel uncomfortable because my ten always surpassed me in everything. My ten realized my jealousy, and he then explained to me that in the country of 2 digits the numbers always work as a team and that what I did was added to what he did. After his explanation, I felt very happy.

11 = 10 + 1

When it was time for lunch. While they gave me a hamburger, my ten received 10 hamburgers. I asked the waitress how she knew who the ten was if the 2 numbers were the same look and the same size.

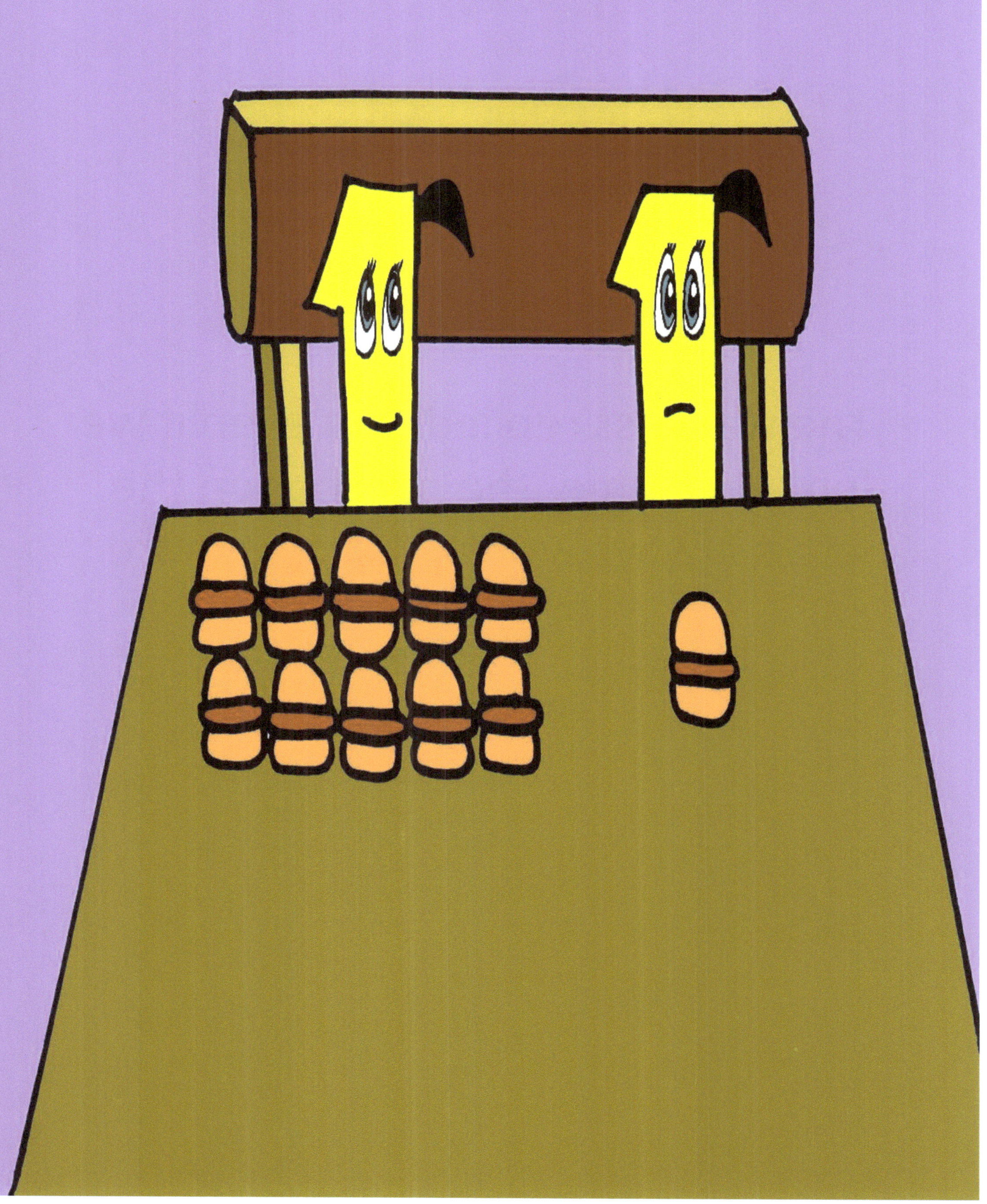

The waitress replied that even if we look the same, the number on the left is always worth 10 times more.

I became close friend with my ten. And even though they always give he more. My ten always shared everything with me. We were a great team in all

It was time to return to our Country of Units. In order to return we had to go through a dividing machine. We were all divided by 11, to make us 11 times smaller and thus we returned to our original value.

Before leaving, my ten told me that he was going to visit us soon.

We crossed the border and got on our plane back home

Back in class, the teacher asked us to write a report on what we liked the most about that trip to the Land of the Tens. Then the teacher showed us the photos that she took with the dozens and us before they put us in the machine that made the numbers all the same size. How small we saw next to them. It was a great experience and I think a great friendship was born between them and us.

END

www.ingramcontent.com/pod-product-compliance
Lightning Source LLC
Chambersburg PA
CBHW042100110726
48006CB00002B/469